The 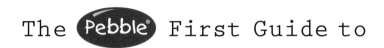 Pebble® First Guide to

Penguins

by Katy R. Kudela

Consulting Editor: Gail Saunders-Smith, PhD

Consultant: Deborah Nuzzolo, Education Manager
SeaWorld, San Diego, California

Capstone
press®

Mankato, Minnesota

Pebble Books are published by Capstone Press,
151 Good Counsel Drive, P.O. Box 669, Mankato, Minnesota 56002.
www.capstonepress.com

1 2 3 4 5 6 14 13 12 11 10 09

..ry of Congress Cataloging-in-Publication Data
Kudela, Katy R.
    The pebble first guide to penguins / by Katy R. Kudela.
       p. cm. — (Pebble books. Pebble first guides)
    Includes bibliographical references and index.
    Summary: "A basic field guide format introduces 13 species of penguins.
Includes color photographs and range maps" — Provided by publisher.
       ISBN-13: 978-1-4296-2242-4 (hardcover)   ISBN-10: 1-4296-2242-3 (hardcover)
       ISBN-13: 978-1-4296-3440-3 (paperback)   ISBN-10: 1-4296-3440-5 (paperback)
       1. Penguins — Juvenile literature. I. Title. II. Series.
QL696.S473K83 2009
598.47 — dc22   2008028233

About Penguins

Penguins are birds that cannot fly. They spend most of their
time in the water. Penguins do spend time on land to raise
their young. The "lives" information in this book focuses on
the land habitat for each of the featured penguin species.

Note to Parents and Teachers

The Pebble First Guides set supports science standards related to life science.
In a reference format, this book describes and illustrates 13 penguin species.
This book introduces early readers to subject-specific vocabulary words,
which are defined in the Glossary section. Early readers may need assistance
to read some words and to use the Table of Contents, Glossary, Read More,
Internet Sites, and Index sections of the book.

Table of Contents

Adélie Penguin

Height: 1.5 to 2 feet (.5 to .6 meter)

Weight: 11 pounds (5 kilograms)

Eats: fish, krill

Lives: nests on rocky islands and ice-free beaches

Facts:
- has white rings around eyes
- builds nest out of pebbles

4

Adélie Penguin Range

Atlantic Ocean

South America

Antarctica

Indian Ocean

Pacific Ocean

☐ Antarctic coastline

adult

chick

African Penguin

Height:	1 to 2 feet (.3 to .6 meter)
Weight:	10 pounds (4.5 kilograms)
Eats:	fish, krill
Lives:	nests in burrows on rocky coasts
Facts:	• grunts like a donkey
	• also called black-footed penguin

African Penguin Range

☐ southern Africa's coastline and nearby islands

chick

Chinstrap Penguin

adults

chicks

Height:	1.5 to 2 feet (.5 to .6 meter)
Weight:	9 to 10 pounds (4 to 4.5 kilograms)
Eats:	fish, krill
Lives:	nests in ice-free areas on rocky coasts
Facts:	• named for line of black feathers under chin
	• also called the bearded penguin

8

Chinstrap Penguin Range

Atlantic Ocean

South America

Antarctica

Indian Ocean

Pacific Ocean

☐ Antarctic Peninsula and subantarctic islands

Emperor Penguin

adult

chick

Height:	3 to 4 feet (1 to 1.2 meters)
Weight:	60 to 90 pounds (27 to 41 kilograms)
Eats:	crustaceans, fish, squid
Lives:	nests on sea ice
Facts:	• largest penguin by weight • male keeps egg warm under his brood pouch

Emperor Penguin Range

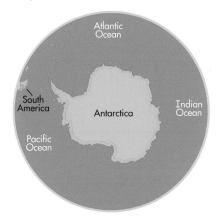

Antarctic coastline

brood pouch

Fairy Penguin

Height:	1 to 2 feet (.3 to .6 meter)
Weight:	2 to 3 pounds (1 to 1.4 kilograms)
Eats:	crustaceans, small fish, squid
Lives:	nests on sandy hills or grasslands
Facts:	• smallest penguin by weight
	• also called little blue penguin

Fairy Penguin Range

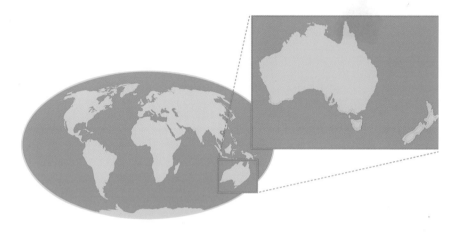

☐ southern Australia and New Zealand

chick

Galápagos Penguin

Height:	1 to 2 feet (.3 to .6 meter)
Weight:	5 to 6 pounds (2 to 3 kilograms)
Eats:	small fish, squid
Lives:	nests on rocky beaches
Facts:	• lives the farthest north of any penguin • holds flippers away from body to stay cool • endangered

Galápagos Penguin Range

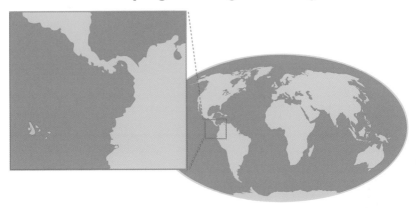

☐ Galápagos Islands

adult

chicks

Height:	2 to 3 feet (.6 to 1 meter)
Weight:	14 pounds (6.4 kilograms)
Eats:	crustaceans, fish, squid
Lives:	nests on grassy or other ice-free beaches
Facts:	• has red-orange bill and feet • has long, stiff tail

Gentoo Penguin Range

Atlantic Ocean

South America

Antarctica

Indian Ocean

Pacific Ocean

☐ Antarctic Peninsula and subantarctic islands

egg

Humboldt Penguin

Height: 2 to 3 feet (.6 to 1 meter)

Weight: 10 pounds (4.5 kilograms)

Eats: small fish, crustaceans

Lives: nests on rocky coasts or in sea caves

Facts:
- creates nest burrows in bird droppings
- also called Peruvian penguin
- endangered

18

Humboldt Penguin Range

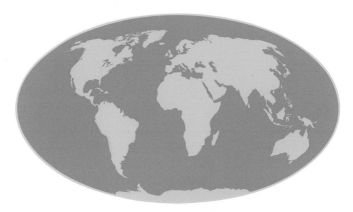

☐ coastal Peru and Chile

young Humboldt penguins

King Penguin

Height:	3 feet (1 meter)
Weight:	24 to 35 pounds (11 to 16 kilograms)
Eats:	fish, squid
Lives:	nests on beaches free of snow and ice
Facts:	• parents hold egg on feet to keep it safe
	• newly hatched chicks have no feathers

King Penguin Range

Atlantic Ocean

South America

Antarctica

Indian Ocean

Pacific Ocean

☐ coasts of subantarctic islands

adult

chick

Macaroni Penguin

egg

Height:	2 to 3 feet (.6 to 1 meter)
Weight:	10 to 11 pounds (4.5 to 5 kilograms)
Eats:	fish, krill, squid
Lives:	nests on rocky coasts
Facts:	• has reddish brown eyes • may lay eggs under plants or rocks

Macaroni Penguin Range

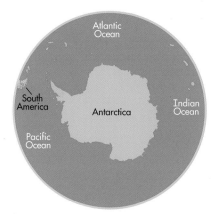

Atlantic
Ocean

South
America

Antarctica

Indian
Ocean

Pacific
Ocean

☐ Antarctic Peninsula and subantarctic islands

Magellanic Penguin   Say It: maj-uh-LAN-ik

chicks

adult

Height: 2 to 3 feet (.6 to 1 meter)

Weight: 11 pounds (5 kilograms)

Eats: fish, krill, squid

Lives: nests along coasts and on islands

Facts: • nests in underground burrows
         or bushes
         • has two black bands across chest

24

Magellanic Penguin Range

☐ coastal Chile and Argentina

Royal Penguin

Height:	2 to 3 feet (.6 to 1 meter)
Weight:	13 pounds (6 kilograms)
Eats:	fish, krill, squid
Lives:	nests on beaches or small grassy hills
Facts:	• male lines nest with grass and stones • only crested penguin with white cheeks and chin

Royal Penguin Range

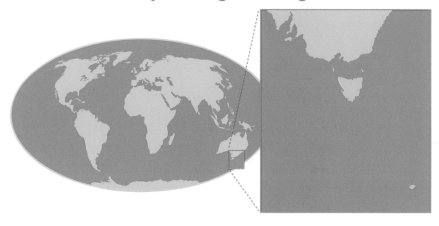

☐ Macquarie Island

Yellow-Eyed Penguin

Height: 2 to 3 feet (.6 to 1 meter)

Weight: 14 pounds (6.4 kilograms)

Eats: fish, squid

Lives: nests in open forests and grassy areas on coastal cliffs

Facts:
- has band of yellow feathers on head
- endangered, fewer than 5,000 alive

Yellow-Eyed Penguin Range

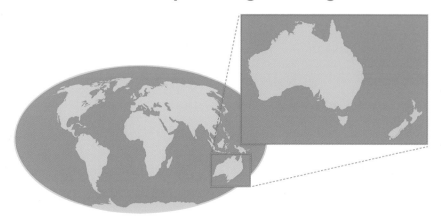

☐ coastal New Zealand and southern islands

chick

Glossary

brood pouch — a warm layer of feathered skin

burrow — a hole in the ground in which an animal lives

chick — a young bird

coast — land next to an ocean or sea

crest — a crown of pointed feathers on a bird's head; penguins with a crest are called crested.

crustacean — a sea animal with an outer skeleton, such as a crab, lobster, or shrimp

dropping — bird waste

endangered — at risk of dying out

flipper — a winglike body part on a penguin; flippers help penguins swim.

krill — a tiny animal that penguins catch in the ocean and eat; krill are similar to shrimp.

squid — a sea animal with a long, soft body and 10 fingerlike arms used to grasp food

Read More

Arnold, Caroline. *A Penguin's World.* Caroline Arnold's Animals. Minneapolis: Picture Window Books, 2006.

Hall, Margaret. *Penguins and Their Chicks.* Animal Offspring. Mankato, Minn.: Capstone Press, 2004.

Internet Sites

FactHound offers a safe, fun way to find educator-approved Internet sites related to this book.

Here's what you do:

1. Visit *www.facthound.com*

2. Choose your grade level.

3. Begin your search.

This book's ID number is 9781429622424.

FactHound will fetch the best sites for you!

Index

Grade: 1
Early-Intervention Level: 22

Editorial Credits
Alison Thiele, set designer; Biner Design, book designer; Jo Miller, photo researcher

Photo Credits
Ardea/Francois Gohier, 25; M. Watson, 10
Bruce Coleman Inc./Erwin and Peggy Bauer, 13; Joachim Messerschmidt, 18;
   John Glustina, 21; John Shaw, 20
Getty Images Inc./Minden Pictures/Christina Carvalho/FLPA, 8; Minden Pictures/
   Konrad Wothe, 19, 26; Minden Pictures/Tui De Roy, 28; The Image Bank/Joseph
   Van Os, 24
iStockphoto/Daniel Perry, 9; Darren Deans, 7 (left); Jeff Goldman, 5; Krzysztof
   Renkaw, cover (macaroni penguin)
Nature Picture Library/Doug Allan, 11; Pete Oxford, 14, 15, 27
© SeaPics.com, 29
Shutterstock/Adrian T Jones, cover (king penguin); Ifstewart, 4; Jan Martin Will,
   cover (emperor penguin); jeff gynane, 7 (right); john austin, 12; John Lindsay-Smith,
   cover (African penguin); Leksele, 17; Pascaline Daniel, 16; Stephen Meese, 6
SuperStock Inc./James Urbach, 23; Tom Brakefield, 22